268.6
R351a ✓
c.2

An Adventure with People

The *"Reading, Writing, and Arithmetic" of Teaching Religion*

By FERRIS E. REYNOLDS

THE CHRISTIAN EDUCATION PRESS
Philadelphia   •   Pennsylvania

Contents

Preface

TWO FACTS STAND OUT IN MY OBSERVATION OF THE religious life of our day. One is the crucial importance of the church school as an agency for promoting and directing religious thought and action. Whatever one's views may be with respect to the separation of church and state, or the place of the home in Christian education, the fact still remains that upon the church school falls most of the burden of teaching religion. The other fact is equally apparent and thought-provoking; namely, that a great part of the teaching in the church school is carried on by lay people.

Placing these two facts side by side will show the reasons for this book. Everything possible needs to be done to encourage and strengthen that supremely important group, the teachers in our church schools. Likewise, everything possible needs to be done to interest new teachers to accept assignments to teach in the church school, and to encourage them to develop their natural gifts.

My purpose, therefore, is a practical one. There is little if any material in these pages for which I can claim any originality. The treatment is neither scientific nor exhaustive. My only authority for the ideas set forth is that vouchsafed to one who has devoted many years to the cause of teaching religion.

More specifically, I have tried to keep in mind the average church school teacher who is responsible for a class of intermediates or young people or married couples or other groups of adults. Many of these teachers are severely limited as to space and classroom equipment. All of them are occupied with vocational, family, and community responsibilities. Yet they would like to do better work in the church school, and to give a more creditable account of their stewardship as Christian disciples. If these pages can help them in any modest way to realize such worthy ambitions, I shall be grateful indeed.

Leadership training schools have done a great deal to strengthen the work of our local church school teachers. This book may serve as an introductory text in standard leadership courses. It does not presume to be more than an introduction. More specific study of particular age groups is strongly urged, as well as the employment of more specialized methods such as audio-visual aids. What I have tried to deal with here are the simple and basic principles and techniques of teaching —the "reading, writing, and arithmetic" of teaching religion.

No effort should be spared to help a new teacher to get started or an experienced teacher to perfect his skill. While the sink-or-swim method of learning may have its value, it is so dangerous that it is seldom used even by swimming instructors. If the prospective church school teacher knows that he will not be plunged into his work by the sink-or-swim method, the administrator will find it easier to recruit new teachers.

In the last analysis staffing the church school becomes a matter of helping people to learn to teach well enough to make them feel that the job is worth while. Once a teacher attains a measure of real competence he will want to continue his teaching. It is the poorly prepared teacher with his halting style of teaching who does not want to remain on the staff.

Although the task is not easy it is certainly good strategy to concentrate upon training competent teachers. Most congregations are made up of people of good intelligence and surely some of them can become effective teachers.

The author hopes sincerely that this handbook for teachers will prove helpful to administrators in staffing their church school.

I should like to extend my gratitude to those students of Elon College who have suffered me to try out on them some of my ideas. I wish also to express my thanks to The Christian Education Press for permission to use material which appeared in the *Youth-Adult Teacher's Quarterly*.

FERRIS E. REYNOLDS

Elon College, North Carolina

Part One: THE ADVENTURE

◇◇

O Thou whose feet have climbed life's hill,
And trod the path of youth,
Our Saviour and our Brother still,
Now lead us into truth.

The call is Thine: be Thou the Way,
And give us men, to guide;
Let wisdom broaden with the day,
Let human faith abide.

Who learn of Thee the truth shall find,
Who follow, gain the goal;
With reverence crown the earnest mind,
And speak within the soul.

Awake the purpose high which strives,
And, falling, stands again;
Confirm the will of eager lives
To quit themselves like men:

Thy life the bond of fellowship,
Thy love the law that rules,
Thy Name, proclaimed by every lip,
The Master of our schools.

—LOUIS F. BENSON

1
Why Teach?

◇◇◇◇◇◇◇◇◇◇◇◇◇◇◇◇◇◇◇◇◇◇◇◇◇◇◇◇◇◇◇◇◇◇◇◇◇◇

WHY SHOULD I COMMIT MYSELF TO TEACHING IN the church school? Surely there are other ways in which I can serve my church. There must be other jobs in the church that will not tie me down so definitely."

Remarks such as this are made every day, and it is true that not everyone in the church needs to feel that he must become a teacher in the church school. Perhaps there is a real sense in which teachers are born to their task. Teaching is a special kind of adventure and not everyone responds to it.

If, however, we deny ourselves the opportunity to experience the excitement and the inner rewards that come from teaching, how are we to know whether or not we are born to the task? Many a pure-bred bird dog, born to hunt the fields and taste the keen enjoyment of autumn trips in the out of doors, has lived and died without pointing a single bird. We, too, do not always get the opportunity to do what we were born to do; or we may fail to grasp the chance when it presents itself.

Teaching Is an Adventure

Until we have given the task a thorough trial, it is hardly fair to assume that we are not born to teach. One day at a swimming pool the writer watched some boys jump off a high diving board. He noticed that before they jumped the less experienced turned their eyes aside first for a stern marshaling of nerve. For them, it was a new adventure, a leap into the blue. So it is with almost any new adventure. All of us can recall how awkward and uncomfortable we felt on our first day of school or the first time we tried to drive a car. Yet, in spite of the awkwardness, who would want to miss all those experiences which call for a leap into the blue.

Values and Rewards of Teaching

Teaching offers certain values and rewards which can be pointed out to the person who has not tried it. It is even possible that some who are already engaged in teaching have not yet become fully aware of them.

THE FEELING OF DOING OUR PART. Each new generation has a right to its religious heritage. The Bible records the process by which the religious values, insights, and discoveries of previous ages were passed on faithfully by each succeeding generation. Others before us took the time and put forth the effort to help our generation to claim its religious heritage. They did their part in this age-by-age assignment. Surely a similar obligation falls upon us toward the members of the next generation. The acceptance of a teaching adventure in the church school brings with it the satisfaction of fulfilling this time-honored obligation.

THE SENSE OF BEING NEEDED. Why is it that we feel embarrassed and chagrined in situations where we do not seem to be needed? It is an established fact that a sense of being needed is a fundamental requirement of human beings for wholesome living. We cannot achieve any real sense of security in this world without a sense of being necessary to someone. A parent who feels that he is not essential to the well-being of his family is an ill and unhappy person. Often without being consciously aware of it the church school teacher is fortified by a sense of being needed by the members of his class, of being necessary to the program of his church and to the purposes of God.

THE JOY OF CREATIVE EFFORT. An artist will deny himself almost anything in order to pursue his chosen work. The true craftsman forgets the passing of time and throws himself into his labors. Creative effort is a partnership with one's Creator. It brings its own rewards of interest and satisfaction. Those who have tasted its sweetness become lifelong devotees of creative work, finding delight in the labors of their hands or their minds. Teaching offers ample opportunity for almost every kind of creative effort. The very challenge of putting old truths into new forms whets the mind of the teacher. In teaching, all of his powers of originality and his gifts of creativity find normal and constructive outlets. The joys he experiences are known only to the members of the select fraternity of creators.

THE PRIVILEGE OF ASSOCIATION. Not many adults have a chance to mingle freely with young people. They become so absorbed in their own adult world that they may fail to realize their lack of fellowship with the young. Even those who have young people in their homes rarely have the opportunity to associate with them in the same way that the church school teacher does. "I would grow old twice as fast were it not for the youngsters in my class at church," one enthusiastic teacher confessed.

Generally speaking, young people do not "open up" or respond to adults. They guard their world against what they consider adult invasion as fiercely as a dog guards his collection of treasured bones. It is a privilege to be invited to share "the long, long thoughts of youth." Happy indeed is the adult who has been fully accepted into the fellowship circle of the younger generation.

To be sure, not all church school teachers are granted this privilege. Accepting the responsibility of a class carries no written guarantee that a teacher will be given the confidence of its members. Still, an effective teacher is more than likely to be "invited in."

A DIRECTED PROGRAM OF STUDY. "I am going to study the Bible and do some other serious reading," is a common New Year's resolution. Yet, how many times does a busy adult carry through such a resolution? In our crowded days there seems to be little time for directed study and self-cultivation. Unless we have a definite purpose, our reading or other literary effort is likely to be spasmodic or entirely lacking. We may begin with high resolves, but before long other demands have claimed our precious moments.

An assignment of teaching in the church school supplies an incentive, a purpose, and a direction for the teacher's study. No longer is his reading done in a hit-or-miss fashion. When he goes to the library he does not need to solicit suggestions for books from the librarian; he needs only to know where he can find the books that will help him in his teaching.

At the end of the year when he begins to look back over his self-adopted course of study, he is gratified to find that he has accomplished something in his spare time. All power tends to atrophy with disuse. The person who is aware of this peril of mental and spiritual stagnation will welcome the motivation that teaching supplies for his personal study program.

GROWTH IN CHRISTIAN DISCIPLESHIP. How many of Jesus' illustrations were concerned with growing things! He compared the reign of God in the individual life to the growth of a mustard seed, to growing grain, to fruit-bearing branches, and the like. Growth of character was regarded as one of the unmistakable signs of true Christian faith. The Gospels and the book of The Acts give us detailed accounts of how the disciples grew and matured in spiritual stature. In the thought of the New Testament, life and growth go together as do the terms "love" and "God." How can we be followers of Jesus unless we continue to grow in understanding, in emotional maturity, and are willing to venture forth toward new horizons of service?

Again and again, teachers claim that they get more out of their teaching than their pupils do; yet, this does not mean that the members of their classes are being cheated. Naturally, teaching contributes to the personal development of the teacher. It would be safe to say that the person who continues to teach effectively in the church school will continue to grow in Christian discipleship. Surely this is a positive value.

Ever since the early days of the Christian Church, to which the writer of the Epistle of James addressed himself, there has been a gulf between the profession and the practice of religion. "Faith apart from works is dead," James affirms. Religious devotion must express itself in the language of action. "Doers of the word," to use another of James' expressions, are those whose faith is made concrete in terms of behavior.

Bridging a Gulf

There are many ways to say, "I love God," but teaching in the church school is one of the most readily available as well as important ways of translating personal religious faith into action. What better or more eloquent way to affirm, "I love God," than to devote ourselves to the task of helping the members of a church school class to find God's will for their lives? When we pray, "Thy kingdom come, thy will be done," our words are not mere pious ritual. In effect, we are saying, "I want God's kingdom to come and his will to be done badly enough to do what I can to help to bring it to pass."

Bridging the gulf between faith and works is not easy. There are always ways to find excuses for turning teaching assignments over to someone else. Following are some familiar objections raised by those who are reluctant to undertake the teaching task, with answers from those who would be "doers of the word" through teaching in the church school.

LET GEORGE DO IT. Passing the buck is an ancient practice that is found even in the church school. But in the church school making excuses involves a matter of

Christian stewardship. Someone has to do the job, and our successor may be not so well qualified as we are, or he may already be performing several other tasks connected with the church program. All too often this is the case. At best the church school teacher can devote only a part of his time to his teaching, but if that part of his time is divided further among other church duties, he can scarcely do his best work. We must consider carefully whether after all the job isn't up to us.

I AM TOO BUSY. "I would like to teach a class, but I am too busy," is a refrain so old and badly worn as to sound like an old phonograph record repeating over and over. Many people who would never make such a remark aloud nevertheless make it to themselves. It is a well-established fact that people find time to do the things they consider interesting or important. One of the reasons that thousands of busy men and women do teach in the church school is that they find their teaching both interesting and important. We might well ask whether anyone who is not busy is capable of teaching.

I AM A FAILURE. "I've tried to teach a class, but I just can't get the hang of it. I rather enjoy it, but there seems nothing for me to do but admit that I'm a failure." This common report may sound discouraging, but actually it holds real promise. The person who makes such a confession may be on his way to becoming an effective member of the church school staff. He has learned that teaching is difficult, but he also has had a sample of the adventure that it offers. He is prepared to make an important investment of time and effort in the business of learning to teach.

Almost any adult in the church who raises the question, "How do you go about teaching in the church school?" is a bright prospect for the teaching staff. The church needs to cultivate its teachers as it does its promising musicians and group leaders. To accept the "I am a failure" verdict as final is always a great mistake.

The Heart of the Matter

If we were to interview a number of recognized religious leaders to find out what factors in their early experience helped to determine the direction of their lives, very likely we would get one story after another of a church school teacher whose influence went far beyond anything that teacher could have imagined. The extent of a teacher's influence is incalculable, yet often it turns out to be a decisive factor in the lives of his students. The very unknown quantity of one's possible influence over the members of his class adds to the excitement of teaching.

Why do literally thousands of men and women devote their time to teaching in the church school week after week? Often those who do not play golf puzzle over the enthusiasm with which their acquaintances apply themselves to the sport. "I can't see how anyone can get excited about chasing a little white ball around through the woods and across the fields!" they exclaim. We never hear such a remark from an ardent golfer. Perhaps the best answer to our question, "Why teach?" is, "Try it and see!"

2

The Teacher and His Task

◇◇

TEACHER IS THE NAME MOST FREQUENTLY USED with reference to Jesus. And what a teacher he was! From the first he seems to have looked upon teaching as his basic work.

Jesus' teaching did not take the pattern used by the scribes and the rabbis, the recognized teachers of his day. Their method was to recite long passages from the Hebrew Scriptures, usually in singsong fashion, together with the interpretations of famous teachers of the past. Often their teaching was dry and unrelated to daily living. Splitting hairs over theological distinctions was their stock in trade. Tradition was their authority and their refuge. With Jesus it was different.

Jesus, the Ideal Teacher

For Jesus, teaching was an adventure, fascinating and full of life. It was the practical side of truth-seeking. The truths he knew were too exciting to keep to himself and his teaching was the result. For Jesus, the truth was a living thing. What he taught was fresh from his own experience of God. It was related to life as intimately as the branches to the vine.

Jesus amazed his hearers by the way he taught. Every word he spoke had meaning for them because it was directed to their experience. They found themselves saying, "That young man is right!" although they could not say exactly why. "He teaches with authority; he is not like other teachers we have heard," was all the explanation they could give.

Jesus did not confine his influence to the minds and the spirits of his hearers. He took them as he found them, body and soul together, respecting their bodies because he respected their souls. Jesus saw that no one with a diseased body or mind could achieve the purpose that God intended him to fulfill in the world. Therefore, he never limited his task to teaching in the strictest sense of the term. Instead, he went about healing all manner of sickness and disease. His ministry was to the whole person, not to any one part. The teeming variety of Jesus' ministry issued from the fact that he recognized the great diversity of human needs.

Is it merely out of piety that we suggest Jesus as the model for the teacher to follow? Hardly! Even those concerned with the more secular phases of education recognize that the teaching of Jesus represents the supreme achievement in that art. Again and again, those who wish to study the methods of teaching turn to Jesus as the unchallenged expert in the field.

It is not enough for us to ask, "What did Jesus teach?" The question, "How did Jesus teach?" is even more important and rewarding. If, before we try to teach any given lesson we develop the habit of asking ourselves, "How would Jesus have taught this lesson?" we make Jesus our model in practice as well as in theory.

At a meeting of sales representatives some of the veteran salesmen were asked to express their opinions on the following questions: "Is it enough for a salesman to know his product in order to sell it?" "How much real salesmanship lies in knowing the customer?" "What knowledge is most important to the ambitious salesman?" The senior salesmen agreed that expert knowledge of a product is not sufficient in itself to assure success in selling it. A salesman must know his customers. No amount of knowledge or skill in any other field can take the place of an understanding of the likes and dislikes, the interests, and the individual peculiarities of the people who will buy the product.

A Look at Our Students

Teachers in the church school can take a leaf from the salesmen's book at this point and ask themselves some basic questions about the people in their classes. What are they like? Can we expect to be successful if we fail to ask ourselves at least this one basic question, and seek the answers continually?

To gain an understanding of our students is not easy, but the quest for such understanding is fascinating. Fortunate is the teacher who has a close friend or relative in the same age-bracket as the members of his class. A nephew or niece, or a neighbor's youngster, as we are able to observe him under a variety of conditions, may be able to provide us with valuable information as to the behavior of the members of our classes.

If we try hard enough most of us can remember something of our own youth. In the process we must make allowances for the many changes that have taken place since our young days. Young people are indeed not what they used to be. But we must not let these differences obscure the more important factors, those that are common to young people in every age. A realistic and sincere examination of the recollections of our own youth will prove to be eminently worth while in our attempt to answer the question, "What are they like, these people who attend our classes?"

In what other ways can we find answers to our question? Contacts with individual members of our classes in their homes, through committee work, in planning social and recreational activities, and the like, are always valuable. One teacher discovered that helping to wash dishes with her students after a church social affair gave her more knowledge of them than any of her class contacts.

A teacher will find it useful to record his observations in a small notebook. Some teachers have developed a card system for recording the progress of their students. The particular method of procedure is for each teacher to determine for himself. The important thing is to keep before us our basic question, "What are they like?" in reference to our students and make every possible use of the answers we find.

A Look at the Teacher

The best place for any teacher who wants to understand his task to begin is with himself. Any forward step that he takes will necessarily be a step from where he is. He may profitably begin by asking: "How do I feel about myself in my role as teacher?" "Do I pose as an authority?" "Do a few years' seniority or experience qualify me for such a position?" "Does the fact that I have been asked to teach a class automatically set me up as a specialist in religion?"

Socrates, one of the world's most effective teachers of ethics, never permitted himself to be called a teacher. He liked to think of himself as a gadfly whose business it was to go about stinging dull minds into activity, arousing thought, or as a midwife whose task it was to deliver noble thoughts from productive minds. Rather than call the young learners around him "students" or "pupils," he insisted upon calling them "associates." Would it be practical for us to hold an attitude similar to that of Socrates toward ourselves and our work with those in our classes?

If he desires it, almost any group will allow the leader to do the thinking for all its members. While this may be flattering to the leader, it is hardly the best way to help the members of the group, for they are thus surrendering the joy of exploring new areas of thought merely to avoid the expenditure of effort needed to set forth on their own individual quests for new truth.

A teacher must avoid yielding to this unspoken conspiracy on the part of the group to let him do their thinking for them. Instead, he must devote much of his time and ingenuity to devising means for helping the members of his class to do their own thinking. The teacher should spare no expenditure of effort toward this end, for once their natural reluctance to throw themselves into the classwork is overcome, teacher and associates alike will enjoy the experience of learning together.

THE TEACHER'S MOTIVATION. A woman who had been active in work with young people, and reasonably successful, too, found her success tapering off and her interest dwindling. Soon she was occupying her time and using her resources in less constructive enterprises. When asked why she had dropped her work with young people, her answer was, "They don't appreciate what is done for them, and neither do their parents!" A note of resentment in her voice betrayed her bitterness about the whole experience.

Is the hope of being appreciated an adequate motive for the church school teacher? Everyone looks for a certain amount of appreciation for his efforts, but appreciation is notoriously late in arriving, when it comes at all. It is something like insurance; one has to have an accident or a loss to collect the benefits. Many of us are only now beginning to appreciate some of the church school teachers that we ourselves have had. We recall, too, that no testimonial dinners were given for the Apostle Paul! If the hope of appreciation is our motive for teaching, our teaching career will be brief. To look at ourselves and examine our own motives honestly is certainly an important part of getting ready for the adventure of teaching.

THE EXAMPLE OF JESUS. When we turn to Jesus' teaching to discover his motives what do we find? Did he expect to be appreciated? Was it the hope of appreciation that helped him through a day of teaching? At Nazareth, at the opening of his ministry there, the people rose up in violence and sought to push him off a steep embankment. When he unveiled to the rich young ruler a vital truth about life, "he became sad." When he restored sanity to a demented man, a delegation invited him to depart from their borders. For the most part his contemporaries did not appreciate the work that the Master did. How much would he have accomplished if he had depended on the hope of appreciation to motivate his work?

What then were the motives that spurred Jesus on in spite of every kind of hostility? When at Nazareth he read from the prophet Isaiah, "He [God] has sent me to preach good news to the poor," he felt that God had called him to his work. Paul was to express the same feeling later in the words, "Necessity is laid upon me."

One of the important motives behind Jesus' teaching, then, was his sense of divine mission. In so far as we feel ourselves a part of the Christian vocation of teaching, we are subject to that same sense of divine calling. When we come to feel that God has called us to "preach good news," we find the strongest possible motive for our teaching.

With Jesus this sense of divine mission was supported by three great loves: love of God, love of people, and love of truth. When the Master repairs to a solitary place for prayer, his words, "Not as I will, but as thou wilt," express his devotion to the Father. The Gospel writer's description, "He had compassion on them, because they were like sheep without a shepherd," shows his love of people, while almost any of his parables shows how his passionate love of truth impelled him to give to that truth the necessary vividness to appeal to human minds.

For us, Jesus' basic motives for teaching are like the

oil in the widow's cruse in the Elisha story: the more we use them, the more abundant they become. Actually, we may be almost unaware that they are influencing us until we begin to give expression to them in acts of devotion. Then we find that the essence of love is service. Love of God, love of people, love of truth deepen in us as they continue to motivate our work. To turn once again to the language of Paul, "Love never ends." It can always be depended on to provide the motive-power for our work of teaching.

When Is Teaching Effective?

When is truth really learned? Is it learned when the student can recite the words and phrases in which he has heard it, or when the student can explain it to someone else? These questions continually confront the teacher.

Can we assume that the members of our classes have truly learned the lesson until they have related its truths specifically to their own experience and activities? A truth that makes no difference in the attitude, the outlook, and the pattern of behavior of the student has not been learned in the fullest sense of the word.

Persistent dealing with the question, "When is a truth really learned?" has led educators to define learning in more inclusive terms. Really to be learned a truth must become a part of the student's way of thinking and living. It must become his in a truly personal sense. Accordingly, to set forth and explain a truth are only a part of the teacher's task; perhaps the easiest part. Relating the truth to the thought and experience of the pupils, getting it woven into the student's pattern of behavior, is the most difficult, and the most significant, part of teaching.

What Are the Methods?

While it is essential to appreciate the demands that teaching makes upon the teacher, this still is not enough. There are other questions to be taken up, such as, "How can assignments be made so that they will be carried out?" "What methods shall we use to relate the truths of the lesson to the experience of the students?" These questions and many others take us into the teacher's workshop, where we may examine his tools and his methods of using them in his work. Effective teaching involves the skillful use of teaching tools as definitely as good carpentry requires the effective use of carpenter's tools.

Part Two: THE TEACHER'S WORKSHOP

We would be building; temples still undone
O'er crumbling walls their crosses scarcely lift,
Waiting till love can raise the broken stone,
And hearts creative bridge the human rift;
We would be building; Master, let Thy plan
Reveal the life that God would give to man.

Teach us to build; upon the solid rock
We set the dream that hardens into deed,
Ribbed with the steel that time and change doth mock,
Th' unfailing purpose of our noblest creed;
Teach us to build; O Master, lend us sight
To see the towers gleaming in the light.

O keep us building, Master; may our hands
Ne'er falter when the dream is in our hearts,
When to our ear there come divine commands,
And all the pride of sinful will departs;
We build with Thee; O grant enduring worth
Until the heavenly Kingdom comes on earth.

—PURD E. DEITZ

3
The Question as a Teaching Tool

◇◇◇

A TEACHER OF PUBLIC SPEAKING ONCE GAVE THIS valuable advice to the members of his class: "When you have finished writing the manuscript of your address, go over it and see how many of your sentences you can turn into questions." There is something friendly about a question. It is a call to a fellowship of hospitable minds. It compliments the person to whom it is addressed, quickening his sense of being an intelligent person.

The Skillful Use of Questions

In the days of high-button shoes, one used a little tool called a buttonhook for fastening them. By putting the hook through a buttonhole in the shoe he could hook a button and draw it through the hole in short order. The question is a kind of present-day buttonhook in the hands of a skillful teacher. Using it, the teacher can reach into the minds and experience of his students.

THE INTRODUCTORY QUESTION. To start the lesson with a question may not always be appropriate, but more often than not a good question makes an excellent springboard from which to plunge into the lesson. The value of such an introductory question is lost, however,

[29]

if the answer is not fairly obvious to most of the members of the class. For example, we want the class to see how Jesus used illustrations to make his truths live in the minds of his hearers. Our first question might be, "How would you go about explaining the causes of rain to a small child?" The answer that we want is, "I would use illustrations of things familiar to the child, such as a boiling teakettle or the sweat that appears on a glass of cold water on a hot day." If this answer does not come right away, we ask another question, such as, "What happens when steam strikes a cold surface?" By asking questions in this way we bring out our point and our students will make a discovery. Not only will they enjoy the exercise, but more than likely they will make the truth they have discovered their own.

WHEN NO ONE ANSWERS. What if the teacher asks a question and no one answers or displays any inclination to answer? Should the teacher then answer his own question? Occasionally, but not as a general rule. If we consistently answer our own questions, the members of the class may take it for granted that all of our questions are rhetorical. Such an impression on the part of the class will make it difficult to stimulate any kind of discussion. Sometimes in this situation it is better to ask the question again in different words. Perhaps it can be phrased so that the answer is more apparent. If this attempt fails, the teacher must try, and try again. Almost any group can be engaged in a discussion if a sufficient number of provocative questions is asked.

USING A SERIES OF QUESTIONS. The teacher may find it useful to develop a series of questions, each new question growing out of the answer to the preceding one, something like this:

Question: *What kind of man was Barnabas?*
Answer: *A good man.*
Question: *What did he do that was good?*
Answer: *He encouraged the people at Jerusalem in Christian living.*
Question: *How did he encourage them?*
Answer: *By being friendly and giving of his means, and by helping them to understand his friend Paul.*

What happens if we do not receive the answers we expect? So long as the discussion is lively and in line with the main intent of the lesson, it will be best to follow through with it. The purpose of our series of questions is to stimulate and direct thinking. It makes little difference whether we arrive by way of our previously marked-out route or by some other, as long as we arrive.

But suppose we are following this procedure and the discussion peters out, or the line of thought veers far wide of the lesson theme, what can we do? If we have a good list of discussion questions, it is a simple matter to raise another question and make a new start. The interest of the class will have been aroused by the excursion they have had and the group will be eager to continue the search for answers to other questions.

THE QUESTION AS A COMPLIMENT. We all enjoy being complimented! Compliments not only contribute to our self-esteem, but they also help to establish friendly and sympathetic relations between persons. A question is a form of compliment. We would not think of asking a question if we did not recognize that the person we address has a contribution to make. Or, to take it the other way around, if we never ask a question, our associates may gather either that we have no need of what they have to offer or that we do not recognize them as intelligent persons. Perhaps this is one reason that people are sometimes embarrassed when they are asked a question. They have been given a compliment! Most people are slightly embarrassed when they are given a compliment, although usually they do not mind this form of embarrassment.

Nothing is worth more to the teacher in presenting the lesson and gaining the regard of the members of his class than a good list of questions, for each question is a compliment. To be sure, the questions must not be asked in the manner of an official investigation, nor must they be put in the manner of a cross-examination. Instead, they should be asked in a conversational way to promote fellowship and common understanding. Used thus, they are worth their weight in gold.

DEALING WITH STUDENTS' QUESTIONS. We can expect our students to ask questions. They will contribute questions to any discussion of which they feel themselves a part. But we can hardly expect their questions to carry the discussion along the line of the lesson theme. More than likely the questions which the students offer will tend to divert the attention of the class to matters unrelated to the lesson theme. Naturally, we should deal with our students' questions as frankly and expertly as we can without allowing the discussion to get out of hand or sidetracked from the main issues of the lesson. There is no special value in merely consuming time with pointless arguments.

FRAMING GOOD QUESTIONS. Someone has said that a question properly asked is more than half answered. If that is so, we should endeavor to state our questions so that they carry their own answers. Naturally, we do not want to underestimate the ability of our students by asking a lot of simple or foolish questions, the answering of which will make no demands upon them. Neither will we gain much by putting our questions so that no one can aswer them. The art of using questions lies somewhere between these two extremes. To master the art is a major achievement in the task of becoming an effective teacher.

Questions Help in Preparation for Teaching

When we apply ourselves to the framing of an extensive list of teaching questions we force ourselves to master the lesson material and make it a part of our own thinking. Even if we do not use any considerable number of these questions in the actual conduct of the class, the exercise will be valuable. The leading issues of the lesson will begin to shape themselves in our minds and our own interest will be heightened. Thus, questions not only may keep our students awake on Sundays, they may keep us awake during our period of preparing the lesson. At first it may appear difficult to make out such a listing of questions. Perhaps our first lists will be brief. But we can increase our skill by making this a kind of game where we try to see how many questions we can find to ask about the lesson and keep our score week by week.

Questions State Facts or Issues

It is possible and often profitable to use questions to affirm facts or beliefs. As we read the Gospel records we can note how often the Master Teacher uses questions to affirm his convictions. For example—"Are ye not worth more than birds?" (Matt. 6:26, *Moffatt*). When Jesus was asked whether it was lawful to pay tribute to Caesar, he countered with the question, "Whose image is on the coin?" With this one question he affirmed the distinction between civic and religious obligations. To put Jesus' answer in declarative sentences we would have to say: "Civic responsibilities and religious obligations are not identical. As a citizen of the state one is subject to the requirements of those in authority in the state. As a religious person, a child of God, one is subject to the authority of God. Because God is supreme over all, his authority is supreme. Certainly he expects his children to be good citizens."

Observe how much more cumbersome and uninteresting this statement is when it is put into declarative sentences. In one swift question the Master set forth a whole paragraph of meaning. But what is more important, he forced his hearers to form their own conclusions. They were not told the answer; they had to make up their own minds. To use questions in this way gives people the satisfaction of reaching their own conclusions, and their conclusions in turn carry additional weight with them because they were reached in this manner. Learning has been a cooperative experience.

4

Making Class Sessions Interesting

◇◇◇

OUR CLASS SESSIONS SHOULD BE PLEASANT EXPERI-
ences. Unless people enjoy the class sessions in
the church school they will not attend. Some children
come to church school regularly because of their home
training, but we are also anxious to reach the youngsters from homes which lack any religious emphasis.
Likewise, it is the adults with no well-formed church-
going habits whom we want to bring into the fellowship of the church school. For these people it is especially important that our class sessions should be interesting.

Moreover, it is a recognized fact that learning, in
order to be enduring and effective, needs to be associ-
ated with a pleasant experience. A person who enjoys
the class sessions will certainly get more out of them
than one who does not. Therefore, we cannot afford to
spare any effort to make our classwork a pleasant experience for all our students.

Make the Job Fun

The attitude of the teacher goes a long way toward
setting the attitude of the group. If the teacher has
thoroughly enjoyed preparing the lesson and looks upon
his teaching as an adventure, more than likely the mem-

bers of his class will share his mood. We must enjoy the teaching task ourselves. Then we can make it fun for our students.

Add a Touch of Humor

A touch of humor is in order; only the type of humor that destroys dignity and reverence is out of place. A true sense of humor is a sense of proportion, a sign of sound physical and mental health. That young people appreciate humor is obvious to anyone who watches a group of them for half an hour and notes their frequent bursts of laughter. We will do well to cultivate the use of the right type of humor in our class sessions.

Use Projects

To undertake projects with our students will add to their enjoyment of the classwork. That people like to do things is evident from the fact that the happiest of them usually seem to have a hobby or two. Often a church school group will get more pleasure out of painting their classroom than from attending a party given especially for them. Projects afford students and teachers the enjoyable opportunity to do things together.

Stimulate Discussion

Lively discussions are a delight to almost everyone. It may be wise strategy for a teacher to start a good heated argument occasionally, to sharpen the edge of his students' interest. As we shall explain later on in this book, when we have prepared our lesson and know what we want to accomplish, we need not be afraid to have a brief excursion of this kind during the class period.

There is some difference of opinion on the question as to whether a class session is a success unless each and every person present has taken an active part in it. Few experienced teachers, however, will deny the primary importance of student participation. They know that learning is give and take, an adventure in fellowship.

Secure Student Participation

The more our students enter into the program of the class the better. In some church schools, in order to insure the maximum amount of student participation, the teacher assumes the role of chairman of the class. He helps with the planning of the class session, assigns the material for study, and otherwise directs the class activities. It is his function to open the session as well as to see that it is closed in some appropriate way. Somewhere between this pattern and the old formal lecture type of procedure, it should be possible for us to arrive at a working balance.

To recognize the importance of student participation is one thing; to get young people to take part in the class program is quite another. Perhaps we have had experiences similar to that of the teacher who complained, "When I ask a question the students sit there like so many bumps on a log." If so, we will value some suggestions that others have found helpful in encouraging students to take part in the church school program.

KEEP THE ATMOSPHERE INFORMAL. To reduce the element of formality in our class sessions is one way of encouraging participation, by putting our students at ease. Often we can do this merely by shifting the chairs and other furniture in the room to make the arrangement look less stiff. Our classrooms should look more like workshops ,and less like meeting halls than they usually do. A friendly attitude and a relaxed manner on our part also will go a long way toward eliminating the stiffness in the atmosphere which so often keeps students from participating in class activities.

HAVE A PLANNED PROGRAM OF ACTIVITIES. If our class session is to be an adventure in fellowship, we need to plan it that way from beginning to end. The use of projects will be helpful in getting this pattern of procedure started. We must let our students know that we are depending on them to help us to develop the lesson. A blackboard will be helpful to write down any suggestions the students may make or any issues they may raise which need to be discussed. When everyone's attention is focused on the blackboard, self-consciousness on the part of individuals is relieved, because what is placed on the blackboard becomes common property.

GIVE INDIVIDUAL ASSIGNMENTS. Individual assignments may serve to engage the interest and participation of the students. In every class some of the members will have special talents and interests. A student who is talented in art might do the drawings or the lettering needed for a certain project. Someone else may have a flair for statistics. Still another person may have access to special sources where he can get valuable information to contribute to the class sessions.

USE COMMITTEES. Committee assignments help to get everyone working on the class program. Often class members will tackle together a problem which they would not attempt as individuals. Suppose one of the lessons will be more vivid with the addition of some information from the welfare department on the matter of broken homes in the community. A committee of three might be delegated to gather that information and present it to the class. The participation of these three committee members in the discussion of this problem will be virtually guaranteed.

Stimulate Curiosity

Unfortunately, in the classic lists of Christian virtues curiosity does not appear. Indeed, it is sometimes mildly condemned as being idle and foolish. Yet, how much truth-seeking would there be without curiosity? How many explorations and discoveries would be made were it not that people are curious? In the work of the teacher this quality can be exceedingly useful. Curiosity leads to truth-seeking. It can add elements of variety and freshness to the class sessions. It may even help to banish the all-too-prevalent impression that church school courses are cut and dried. Because people are curious, they will feel closely bound to the teacher who shares their curiosity.

Create Mental Pictures

Why does advertising make such extensive use of pictures? How much goods would a mail-order house sell if it did not picture the articles in its stock in a catalog? People's minds are stimulated by pictures. An idea is a mental picture or series of pictures. Through a picture the advertiser gives his customer the idea he wants him to have.

It is easy enough to present a picture of an object such as a house or a cow, but it is a different matter to attempt to picture a quality such as love, justice, or mercy. Probably the best way to picture these less objective matters is to associate them with the faces, hands, or feet of living persons. Although it is difficult to picture mercy, it is not difficult to picture a person acting with mercy.

The teacher is constantly confronted with the question, "How can I help my students to get mental pictures that are clear and vivid?" Often when students appear to be uninterested it is because what is going on in the class fails to suggest any pictures to their minds. Suppose we are teaching a lesson about Jesus by the seaside. He is talking with the fishermen. He has a work for those fishermen to do that is far more important than catching fish. Here are interesting pictures aplenty.

We must help our students to see the boats with their strange rigging, the nets, and the swarthy fishermen. Unless we can make the disciples become real people for the members of our classes, their lives will have little force for our students. Living people are interesting. If the members of the class can see the fish scales on Simon's clothing and the expression of amazement on his face as, at Jesus' command, he pulls in the net full of fish, they will associate the truths of the lesson with colorful mental pictures.

Teach from Actual Situations

"What is in your hand?" God said to Moses when the latter shrank from the assignment he had been given to lead the people of Israel out of their bondage in Egypt.

But when Moses answered, "A rod," God proceeded to show him how to use what he had to accomplish the work assigned to him.

This Old Testament story may serve as a kind of parable to illustrate an effective way to make our teaching vital and effective, by using actual situations that arise in our class discussions to relate Christian truth to daily living. For example, something in the lesson provokes a discussion of some friction that has developed between the older and the younger people in the church. Members of the class may take advantage of the discussion period to vent their feelings over their grievances, real or fancied. (How far we should permit that sort of thing to go, of course, is a delicate question.) If the teacher is on the alert, he may be able to redirect the thinking of the class with a question or a suggestion. Suppose some student makes the assertion that the older people in the church do not allow the young people to do anything. We must be prepared to point out certain obvious exceptions. We might say, for instance, "How about Mr. Benedict? He is always pulling for the young people."

If we are prepared for such a turn in the discussion we may actually use it to illustrate and drive home the central point of the lesson. We might ask such questions as: "What is the result of the tension between the older people and the younger people in the church?" "What causes the tension?" "How can we proceed to eliminate it?" "Does faultfinding do any good?" "Is name-calling a Christian act?" "What is the positive approach to this problem of friction between generations?"

Very often teaching out of a situation such as this is

the most effective kind of teaching. Of course, the teacher runs the risk of failing to get out of the situation! However, the teacher who knows his class and is thoroughly prepared need not worry overmuch about taking a chance. A situation like this presents one of the challenges that make teaching fun.

How much of Jesus' teaching was "out-of-a-situation" teaching! Two brothers quarreled about their inheritance. Jesus used their situation to set forth the ideal attitude toward wealth and the problems of covetousness. When there was contention among the disciples about who was the greatest, Jesus seized the opportunity to set forth the meaning of true greatness.

Provide a Program of Activity

"Skull-practice" is a term for that part of the training of athletes for competitive sports when the various plays are diagramed and rehearsed, usually on a blackboard. The coach knows the value of these sessions, but he never would think of making them a substitute for practice on the field. Perhaps the severest challenge that a teacher faces is the need to provide opportunities for the practice of the truths and principles that are taught in the church school sessions. Can we assume that "skull-practice" alone will serve to develop people who are skilled in the arts of Christian service?

Service projects and programs of activity must constitute a part of our teaching if we are to accomplish our aims. Space, materials, and time impose serious limitations on our use of teaching projects, yet we must not allow these limitations to hinder us from using programs of activity. Is it not better to teach a few of the great Christian truths well than to rush hurriedly through a multitude of them? Often pupils become so interested in a project that they themselves find additional time to work on it. Such projects and activities may be classified roughly as follows:

1. *Projects specifically related to the theme and the material of the lesson.* Maps, charts, slides, scrolls, notebooks, collections, and so on, belong in this group.

2. *Programs and activities that may grow out of the lesson studies,* such as dramatizations, homemade movies, observation tours, conferences with interesting persons. Examples of this group of projects include a visit made by a class that was studying the social teachings of Jesus to all the social agencies in their community and the subsequent discussion of the work of these agencies in the light of Jesus' ministry to people; or, the 32-mm. movie of an interpretation of the parable of the talents made by another church school class.

3. *Committee reports in special areas.* In this kind of project the results of special interviews and observations are brought into the class discussions by smaller groups who have made a special study in some particular area. Most communities have outstanding specialists, such as doctors, lawyers, civic officials, nurses, and educators who are glad to be of service.

Public relations, meaning at its best "helping each other to understand each other," is becoming an important expression in our modern vocabulary and is developing rapidly in many communities. Why should we not take advantage of it in our teaching? Ours is an age of experts and specialists. A few words from a nurse or a doctor or a social worker on the problem of alcoholism, for example, naturally will carry more weight than the opinion of a nonexpert. These committee activities have the added value of helping the members of our classes to locate facts for themselves.

4. *Service projects.* These may be related to the actual Sunday-by-Sunday classwork in only a general way. They may point in many directions. The local church and its program offers many opportunities for classes to take over certain necessary routine jobs, such as cleaning, painting, ushering, mimeographing, and the like. Any community project that challenges the class as a group to express their Christian devotion in terms of action is highly desirable. Activities that reach even farther into the world of human need are also essential if we are to make real to our students the world-wide mission of the Christian Church. When Christian motives and ideals are thus given normal outlets, steady spiritual growth is assured.

5

Illustrations Are Valuable

◇◇

JESUS WAS FOND OF USING BRIEF PARABLES TO POINT out the truth he wanted to teach and to make sure that it would take root in the lives of his hearers. For the church school teacher to overlook or to neglect to use illustrations is to court failure in his teaching. Almost any lesson needs illustrations that have been selected carefully to bring its truth within reach of the members of the class.

Relating Ideals to Experience

Many lessons are planned to develop a particular attitude in the minds of students. For this very reason such lessons may run the serious chance of becoming high and lifted up above the living issues of daily experience. It is easy for anyone to become so enamored of beautiful words and ideals that he has only a vague impression of the truths behind them.

One of the best methods of relating the ideal of the lesson to actual experience is the use of illustrations. A certain minister's life and career were ruined by a vicious and untrue story circulated about him. No bodily injury was inflicted on him; yet he died of a broken heart. Could the person who started that story be considered a murderer? An illustration such as this, used to

[45]

open the discussion of the commandment, "Thou shalt not kill," provides a fresh, down-to-earth approach and prevents the discussion of this topic from becoming threadbare and trite.

Tying the Unfamiliar to the Familiar

How does an illustration work? What mental process does it call into action? An illustration, an example, or an instance—all are different types of the same thing—appeals to the experience of the hearer. It sets before his mind a picture that is familiar, that is related to his experience. To use in a slightly different way an illustration that we have already cited in another connection, let us consider how we might try to explain the process of rain formation to a small child. We might call his attention to the steam that forms on the mirror in the bathroom after his bath. He watches it form into drops of water like rain. Using what he has experienced we can then explain to him the process of cloud formation and rainfall. If our illustration has functioned properly, it has related the truth we wanted to teach to the child's previous experience. When such a truth is effectively related to anyone's experience, it becomes his own. The Master Teacher knew this when long ago he used in his teaching so many stories and parables dealing with familiar things.

Finding Illustrations

Where does the teacher find his illustrations? Do they grow on trees? They did for the prophet Jeremiah. When he saw the almond tree bursting into bloom (Jer. 1:11), it became for him an illustration of God's patient care. Just as the Lord of creation had cared for the embattled tree during the hard winter months and then provided it with a new upsurge of life, so he would take care of his people, Israel.

Sometimes the best illustrations seem to find us. Experiences of almost any kind may give us the material for illustrations. At first we may feel that we need a great many experiences to produce even one effective illustration, but before long, with care, alertness, and practice on our part, they will seem literally to grow on trees, leap from the fields, walk out from streets and alleys. Such familiar sights as a group of children playing house in the back yard may remind us that family life is basic in our civilization; or, two dogs fighting over a bone may point up the problem of material goods and human relations.

Some areas of experience may prove to be more productive of illustrations than others. Much will depend upon the individual teacher and his range of interests. Below are some of these areas that have proved to be the most fruitful for producing illustrations. Here again, in making these suggestions we are taking our cue from Jesus, the Master Teacher.

OBSERVATIONS OF PHYSICAL NATURE. Growing plants and living things catch and hold the interest of most of us. We need not be scientists or experts in agriculture to have a store of knowledge of the world about us. Even those of us who live in large cities have more contact with nature than we realize. "The School of the World," as one thinker called it, is one of our largest educational institutions. Mother Nature has a wonderful way of illustrating her lessons in color and rhythm. Sometimes she wraps her truths in fleecy blankets of snow; again she traces them in stars against the black vault of the heavens.

Animals and insects, too, offer many fine illustrations that will elicit a lively response in the minds of our students; for instance, the spider that encouraged an ancient warrior king to carry on his crusade by its persistence in spinning its web. Ants are fascinating little creatures who get along well together and accomplish almost incredible feats. Birds, mice, bees, fish, as well as household pets, also afford living illustrations of truth.

OBSERVATIONS OF PEOPLE. The affairs of our fellow-men also offer a wealth of illustrative material. Our associates in family life, community enterprises, and business may suggest valuable illustrations to us. The activities of children and young people, at work and at play, reveal and illustrate important truths about life.

To be sure, in drawing upon the activities of people for illustrative material, we must guard against making any possible reflections on personal character or inroads on private matters. The very manner in which a teacher handles his observations of people may be in itself a continuous illustration of respect for personality and zealous care for safeguarding human values.

ILLUSTRATIONS BASED ON CURRENT EVENTS. Illustrations based on contemporary events and movements have a special timeliness. The news is an important feature of everyday experience. The large amounts of money paid to those who undertake to interpret the events in the news witness to the widespread interest of people in what is going on in the world. While we can overwork this area in our search for illustrative material, we do not want to ignore it.

EXAMPLES FROM LITERATURE. Almost all forms of literature, and especially biography, provide the teacher with fresh illustrations. Here again the basic interest of people in what other people do and think, and in the way in which they meet the issues of life, gives such illustrations a special appeal. It is significant that the life stories of baseball players, business men, doctors, scientists, and statesmen are among our best sellers. Almost any good biography will provide the teacher with dozens of vivid illustrations.

MECHANICAL INVENTIONS. Ours is an age of mechanical inventions. Most of us have grown up with machinery and electrical appliances. Engines, storage batteries, cameras, movie projectors, and the like, suggest a great variety of illustrations. For instance, an electric motor may be capable of delivering 5 h.p., but unless it is geared to do a useful piece of work its power provides nothing but lost motion. By the same token, each individual has a certain amount of power to use, but unless he gears his power to some useful task, the result is lost motion.

AUDIO-VISUAL AIDS. The old saying, "Seeing is believing," expresses our great dependence on the sense of sight in learning. The words, "I see," mean, "I understand." The earliest forms of writing were pictures and diagrams. Sometimes students seeking to understand our explanations will say, "Draw us a picture of what you mean."

All of this suggests a source of illustrative material that is truly vast and exciting—the appeal to the eye. Often a simple figure or diagram placed on the blackboard will do wonders in putting across an idea to a class. One need not be an artist to achieve this. It is surprising what can be done with a few representative lines and dots. For example, one way to teach a parable might be to draw two parallel lines on the board to represent the two levels of meaning in the story. The lower line may be used to indicate the everyday factual events of the story, and the upper line to set forth the spiritual truth which it is intended to convey.

Such a teaching method has at least three additional advantages. The instant that a mark or a dot is made on the blackboard attention will be attracted and focused at that point. We have only to try this as a matter of experiment and observe the results. When attention is directed toward any kind of visible object, self-consciousness is eased in both teacher and pupils. A person who would be "scared to death" to make a public address can show the pictures that he took on a trip and tell about them at length without any feeling of nervousness. In addition, there is a wholesome kind of informality which accompanies the use of various aids to vision. Individual experiences of members of the class become group experiences with this method in a way difficult to achieve by any other.

What are some of these aids to vision and how can the teacher secure them? Mention has been made of the more or less impromptu drawings which the teacher and the class may work out together. They may also work on maps, charts, and bulletins as projects related to lesson study. One class studying the Old Testament prophets produced a chart showing the development of the idea of God in the prophetic writings. Another class enlarged a printed chart which pictured the world powers that figured in the development of the Hebrew nation. Printed maps showing the locations of places and events are also important aids for helping students to visualize situations.

Great strides have been made by the various denominational agencies which provide the materials and the equipment for using audio-visual aids, such as slides, filmstrips, and motion pictures. In almost every community there are persons who use audio-visual equipment in their own homes. Audio-visual aids and equipment are now within the reach of even the smallest and most remote churches. Church agencies are eager to help church school teachers and officers to make the fullest possible use of audio-visual aids.

We want to urge here that these audio-visual materials be carefully selected and incorporated into the lesson plans. Suppose our current lessons deal with Paul's work of establishing churches among the Gentiles. It is difficult for present-day students to visualize those situations where the Apostle faced the superstition and the idolatry of his age and the hostility of his own people. A filmstrip showing Paul's missionary journey to Galatia would help the class to see the real nature of these problems and the manner in which the Apostle sought to meet them.

Bulletins and catalogs issued by the denominational

bureaus of audio-visual aids classify and describe the materials which are available, so that it is a simple matter to make the proper selections and work them into the lesson plans.

USING IMAGINATION. Imaginary instances and situations may be used to bring home the truths of the lesson to the members of our classes. Questions such as these may prove provocative: "Suppose an enemy soldier compelled you to carry his bedroll for a mile. How would you feel?" "How do you suppose those people felt who heard Jesus deliver the words of his Sermon on the Mount?"

Most persons welcome an opportunity to use their imagination. When the teacher provides such an opportunity he is likely to get an enthusiastic response. He should be prepared for a wild excursion into the realms of fancy, however, for once the imagination of a group is released, one imagined situation leads to another. Ordinarily, however, our teaching suffers more from the use of too little imagination than from too much!

Choosing Suitable Illustrations

From our outline of sources of illustrative material it is apparent that the familiar question, "Where can I find illustrations?" becomes instead, "How can I choose illustrations from the vast store of common experience?" Eventually illustration-hunting develops in us a kind of special alertness in relation to all our personal contacts. Then, with our continually growing supply of illustrations, selecting those that are the most effective for our immediate purpose becomes our chief problem. How are we to decide what illustrations to employ in a given teaching situation? A few simple principles may help to guide us in making our selections:

Is it clear? We must be sure to choose an illustration that is clear. If we find that a great deal of explanation is necessary to make an illustration serve our purpose, usually it is better to find another where the point is more evident.

Is it brief? Brevity or economy is another guidepost to follow. Observe the brevity of most of the parables of Jesus:

> The kingdom of heaven is like leaven which a woman took and hid in three measures of meal, till it was all leavened (Matt. 13:33).

Even in the longer parables detail is kept at a bare minimum. The thread of meaning may be lost if an illustration is long drawn out. Lengthy stories may be interesting, but their usefulness for illustrative purposes will be enhanced if they are condensed into a few short sentences. If it is impossible to do this with the example we have chosen, perhaps we should look for another. In listening to someone else using an illustration, we may remember feeling the temptation to shout, "Why don't you get to the point!"

Is it of general interest? Scope of interest is another principle of selection. Some illustrations involve specialized knowledge and experience. They may be of great interest to one or two persons in the group, but fail to stir the others. In order to serve its purpose an illustration must be within the scope of experience of most of the members of the group. It is well, too, to select an illustration that will strike the point of keenest interest. With a group of young people an illustration involving movie stars will be more likely to meet with a keen response than one involving the stars of the firmament.

Is it timely? Timeliness is another principle of selection. Different areas of experience claim the limelight at different times, when everyone's attention is focused upon them. For instance, people are always interested in the latest model of a car or other machine. Illustrations involving red-hot areas have a special appeal. To be sure, there are dangers in the exploitation of up-to-the-minute topics and events. We must not allow our church school classes to become mere current events forums. Neither should we retreat into the shadows of antiquity.

Are our illustrations varied? Variety still is the spice of life. We may easily overdo taking illustrations from one particular area. It is so easy to draw too much upon our own field of interest. Illustrations from animal life are effective when used occasionally, but the class that is taken to the zoo every week may eventually object. A teacher who has photography for a hobby must guard against boring his students with his experiments in taking pictures. Travel experiences may provide the teacher with many fine illustrations, but unless he observes the principle of variety, his students will be likely to ask each other, "Where do you suppose he will take us today?" The expression, "When I was in

Europe," shrinks in value for illustrative purposes with each repetition.

Ways of Using Illustrations

COMBINING QUESTIONS AND ILLUSTRATIONS. One good way to use illustrations is to solicit the help of the class in developing them. Suppose we want to use an illustration to show the relation of worship to our inner lives, and that we want to use a comparison involving a storage battery. We might ask questions such as: "What happens inside a storage battery when it is being charged?" "How is electric energy stored in the cells of the battery?" In this way the outline of our illustration will take form from the contributions of the members of the class. Once it is clearly before their minds we may suggest the point we want to make, that worship serves as a recharging process for our inner lives.

USING ILLUSTRATIONS THOUGHTFULLY. Like a sway-backed horse, any illustration may break down if it is loaded too heavily. The hymn-line, "Thou art the potter, we are the clay," illustrates a sound relationship between God and his people. But there are many respects in which people do not resemble clay. For one thing, they are responsible agents with the power to make choices. If the illustration is pursued too far, it may break down or actually convey a false conception of the total relationship of people to their God and Creator.

MAKING BIBLICAL SITUATIONS LIVE. The story told in the Gospels occurred so long ago that the language of the writers and the historical setting of the events are vastly different from those of our own time. Present-day students often find it difficult to picture those events as having actually happened. The teacher must make every effort to help his students to bridge the centuries that lie between our own time and that of the Gospel narratives. He will find it helpful to use as illustrations modern parallels to biblical happenings. He might use an imaginary situation such as this: "Suppose you went to your church some Sunday and found that the vestibule had been turned into an auction market where crosses, candles, and the elements of communion were being sold? When Jesus went to the temple at Jerusalem he found conditions that were even more alarming to the people of his day. What did he do about them?"

A pictorial introduction of this kind may help to bridge the gulf between the biblical account of Jesus cleansing the temple and the customs of our time.

Or, we might take another example. Perhaps the Scripture lesson one Sunday brings together two well-known biblical characters, Zacchaeus and the rich young ruler. In reading over the Scripture account, try to help your students gain a personal acquaintance with both the young ruler and with Zacchaeus. Try to see the troubled earnestness in the face of the young man as he rushes up to Jesus to make his request. Or, see if you can envision him as a young boy living in a home where there was an abundance of material things, where possessions were a frequent topic of conversation. Do you find it possible to feel toward him as the Master did? Attempt to state his personal problem in terms of to-day's experiences.

Ask your students to tell you what sort of person they imagine the Jericho tax collector to have been. The Gospel writer has contributed many suggestions that may help us to gain a picture of him. We find that he was a man of small stature, nimble enough to climb a tree. The writer also emphasizes Zacchaeus' curiosity. The Master found in him a free and enthusiastic spirit and a generous heart. Picture the expression upon the tree-sitter's face when he hears Jesus pronounce his name! The more vivid your mental pictures of both of these men, Zacchaeus and the rich young ruler, and the events in which they figured as they are described in the Gospel accounts, the more interesting the lesson will be for both you and your students.

Living with the great personalities of the Bible is an especially valuable experience for the teacher. Not only does it inspire and enrich his personality, it enables him to present biblical material in a vivid and firsthand manner. The barrier of history is broken down and the persons of the Bible become contemporaries for the teacher and, through him, for the members of his class.

ACTING OUT BIBLE STORIES. To act out the stories of Bible characters may help our students to know the people of Bible times as intimately as they know their contemporaries. The popularity of biblical novels and dramatizations testifies to popular interest in these people of long ago.

In connection with a study of the parables of Jesus, it might be helpful to ask the members of your class to act out some of the more familiar parables. It might add zest to the assignment to ask one section of the class to do the acting while the others try to identify the stories. If the performance merits it, you might work out an arrangement with the superintendent for the assembled church school to see the dramatization.

Further Suggestions to the Teacher

Some teachers find it useful to keep a small notebook in which to jot down suggestions for illustrations. In the rush of daily activities it is not easy to recall an idea that flashed into our minds a month or even a few days back. If we can devise a system of getting such inspirations written down, our percentage of loss will be reduced substantially.

When it is not possible for us to jot down suggestions on the spot, we will find it profitable to set aside a few minutes at the end of the day for a quick review of the day's experiences in an effort to gather up and take possession of the illustrative material which that day has presented to us. Indeed, such a retreat to gather up and make our own the illustrations from the day may be profitably combined with our personal devotions. What better devotional exercise could we employ than to review the past day in the presence of God! Each teacher will need to work out the mechanics of his own procedure, adjusting it to his particular temperament and occupation. The important thing is to gather up and possess each day as much fresh illustrative material as possible.

6

Preparing the Lesson

◇◇◇

COMPARE THE LENGTH OF TIME REQUIRED TO COOK a good dinner with the sixty minutes or so that it takes the family to eat it, or recall that in athletics a good team puts in at least two hours of practice for each minute of actual playing-time. Ought we to be offended or surprised if we run into the same situation when we discover that a church school lesson that can be taught in half an hour requires many hours of preparation? A writer spends years of study and work on a book that can be read in a few hours. A choir spends weeks rehearsing the Easter music that takes only a few minutes to perform on Easter Sunday morning.

Watch the housewife getting ready for her special dinner. Is she bored as she goes about her duties? Does she begrudge every minute she is obliged to spend in the kitchen? Not at all! She is having the time of her life. The hours slip by so quickly that she wonders where the time has gone. It is the same with the team, the writer, or the choir. Often the preparations are more fun than the event itself. Happy is the teacher who enjoys his preparations for teaching, for whom his work is a joy and not a chore!

Attitudes Are Contagious

A trainer of fine bird dogs knows that the attitude of the man handling the dog at a trial often determines the winner. A sensitive dog can be discouraged from doing his best by the indifference or bad temper of the man directing him. The same thing is true of a teacher and his students. The attitude of the teacher is contagious. Often poor training and limited ability in a teacher are far outweighed in the eyes of his students by his eagerness, good humor, and affection for his work. By the same token a competent teacher may fail because he lacks zest, alertness, and an even temper.

"Mighty Are His Preparations!"

"Mighty are his preparations!" is a description of a certain fisherman getting ready for an expedition. A beehive is a quiet place compared with his household when such activities are going on. Rods, reels, lines, hooks, outboard motor, and dozens of other items of equipment and gear are carefully assembled. The type of fishing, the season, and the location must be considered. The omission of even a small piece of tackle might ruin the entire trip; yet he does not want to take along a lot of unnecessary stuff. Practice, care, and experience all contribute to the success of these preparations. The veteran sportsman knows how important they are for a really enjoyable trip, while the spectator may be amused at such an apparent waste of time.

This same phrase, "Mighty are his preparations!" might also be used to describe the preliminary occupations of the teacher who is getting ready for an adventure in teaching. Indeed there are many similarities between the two procedures. The inexperienced or casual observer can hardly be expected to appreciate the importance of these preparations, for to him teaching looks like a simple matter. After all, it is just telling people things that they do not know or explaining things that they do not understand. The answers are all in the book; all the teacher does is to give them out as he might provisions across the counter at a country store. Why are such elaborate preparations required to carry out such a routine function?

Those who have done some teaching know that it is not a routine affair; it is much more like an expedition. To be unprepared for it is like going fishing without a line or a rod. The preparations call for a purpose and the imagination to select in advance the equipment that will be most useful in realizing it. Furthermore, we can never be sure just what sort of situation we may find. Students who have been dull and lifeless for several Sundays may suddenly be brought to a high pitch of interest by some event that has taken place in the community. One teacher brought his class of young people to their feet in a burst of interest when he used the facts of a game-fixing scandal in his neighborhood about which he had taken the trouble to inform himself.

Types of Preparation

Three types of preparation are needed by the teacher in the church school:

1. General cultivation of thought and experience, slanted toward the task of teaching.

[61]

2. Long-range planning of the lessons for the quarter.
3. Preparation of each individual lesson.

It is difficult to say which of these is the most important. All three are essential. Perhaps those most easily overlooked are the first two. For these especially, certain specific procedures may be suggested. Planned systematic reading of good religious literature and the use of various devotional guides will be found highly rewarding. The study of poetry and pictures and the reading of denominational publications should also be worked into the teacher's program of preparation. Teaching is not so much a matter of handing out factual knowledge as it is the sharing of thought and experience. We can hardly hope to share unless we first make every effort to possess an abundance.

Hints on Effective Preparation

START EARLY IN THE WEEK. Does your mind work well under the stress of a time limit? Ask someone a question and give him just ten seconds to answer it. Probably he will fail. Then ask him another question and let him answer at his leisure, and he will probably answer in less than ten seconds. What makes the difference?

Most of us do not think well under pressure. Apparently our minds do their best work when they are not pressed for time. This means something for our work as teachers. It means that the more leisure we can give ourselves in our preparations the better. By looking over the lesson and getting its purpose in mind as early as possible we give our minds a better opportunity to function creatively.

We may be amazed at the number of interesting items that relate themselves to the lesson theme in our minds as we go about our routine activities for the week. Experiences of the farm, shop, or office, items from newspapers or magazines, and the like, will find their way into our lesson preparation. Some teachers find it useful to carry a little notebook for the special purpose of recording lesson hints, ideas, and illustrations which may suggest themselves. At the beginning of the week they jot down the main points of emphasis in the lesson. Then, whenever some item of interest comes up, they enter it in the notebook at the first opportunity. Later in the week, when he confronts the definite job of preparing the lesson, the teacher finds that he is already well along with the task.

HAVE A DEFINITE TIME FOR PREPARATION. "Where can I find the time to prepare the lesson?" is a question raised by almost every teacher. The more emphasis we place upon our preparation the more unyielding and persistent the question becomes. Most of us live on a fairly close schedule. To make room in it for lengthy teaching preparations seems like trying to cover a full-size bed with a three-quarter size sheet. However, most of us have long since found it impractical to try to do all that can or needs to be done. Instead, we have developed the practice of choosing the most important items and letting the rest go. Within a schedule set up on such a basis there is freedom.

Not all the demands upon our time are of equal weight, so that finding time for our teaching preparations becomes a matter of choice. Therefore, the real question becomes, "How important is this demand on our time?"

What about the wisdom of trying to fit our teaching preparation into our schedule at dull or vacant periods, trying to work it in where we can, if we can? Any hit-or-miss method is likely to miss! Scheduled activities have priority. Certainly there is a definite advantage and value in setting aside a specific period of time each week for our teaching preparations. Some teachers find it advisable to divide their allotted time into two or three periods during the week. The teacher will find that this practice keeps him from experiencing any sense of "drag." He will not find himself saying wearily, "It is late in the week. When am I going to get a chance to study my Sunday school lesson?" The self-torture reflected in such a remark need never be endured by the teacher who has a definite time for his class preparation.

HAVE A DEFINITE PLACE ALSO. It is a distinct advantage to have a specific place for one's scheduled activity of lesson preparation. A carpenter does his best work in his own workshop. Hobbyists of all stripes have their special places of retreat.

One advantage of having such a special place is that we often save valuable time that otherwise might be spent in gathering materials together. If we keep these in one place, they are there when we need them each week. Indeed our books, magazines, quarterlies, clippings, and the like, seem to be gathered around us like ministering angels to help us in our weekly assignment.

Probably the first step to take in the preparation of a given lesson is to gain a general acquaintance with the theme, beginning with such questions as, "What is the lesson about? With what specific issues does it deal?"

Step by Step

After a few minutes of this we can go on to the next step which raises the question, "What are the specific needs of the members of the class in relation to the theme of this lesson?"

The answers to the first question may be found in the teacher's book and in the suggested Scripture, but the answer to the second lies in the teacher's own understanding of the people with whom he is working. It is at this point that the important difference between teaching *lessons* and teaching *individuals* comes into our purview. For Jesus, individual needs were primary. He sought to bring the truth to bear on the specific problems of individuals. When two brothers were about to become enemies over the division of their inheritance, the Master dealt with covetousness in terms of the need presented by the brothers.

Here the teacher's knowledge of his students becomes important. If he knows the minds of his associates in his class—their doubts and fears, their strengths and their weaknesses, the difficulties with which they are in daily combat, he will be able to focus the lesson so as to illumine these issues with telling accuracy. In his mind he may call the roll of his class, asking himself the following questions with respect to each individual: "What should this theme mean to him?" "At what point does it come into contact with his particular needs?"

Only after answering these questions to ourselves can we proceed with the preparation of the lesson with the assurance that our efforts will not become lost in pious vagueness. Because the great Christian themes deal with the foremost issues of life, we may rest assured that they can be brought to bear on the needs of individuals once we determine precisely what those needs are.

Mastering the Lesson Material

Most of us require time and diligent application to master our lesson material. Many teachers find it helpful to get an over-all picture of the lesson in their minds early in the week and then to give it time to "soak in." By the time they get to the actual task of preparing the lesson, they find that it has already begun to take shape in their minds. Events of the week, suggestions, and even illustrations, have gathered in support of the lesson theme. Instead of teaching off the surface of their minds these teachers draw their material from deeper strata. Usually the teacher requires time to make the lesson his own, but when it has become a part of his experience, he has mastered it. He uses the material in the Scripture text, in the teacher's and the pupil's books, and that gathered from other sources as he would the tools in his shop. These materials become his servants. As the accomplished pianist finds the keys of his instrument responding to his creative touch without demanding his attention, so the teacher who has mastered his lesson and made it his own finds himself using it with skill.

We may be tempted to be lax in preparing a certain lesson because the material is "old stuff." However, the fact that it has been dealt with many times before makes careful preparation even more necessary. Unless we prepare to use originality, vivid illustrations, and pertinent applications in our presentation the members of our class may also get the feeling that it is "old stuff," and an important lesson will have failed.

The most familiar parts of the Bible, such as the Sermon on the Mount and Paul's famous chapter on love, never cease to inspire fresh thinking in minds that are open and eager. Nothing in the Bible is old stuff unless we assume that it is. To skip over a passage just because the first sentence or two may sound familiar is to deprive our students of appreciating the force and clarity which have made such passages famous. A wiser plan for us is to take time to re-examine the passage with the mental questions: "Why have these words become so familiar? Have I missed anything in my previous reading of them?"

7

The Lesson Plan

◇◇

A LESSON PLAN IS TO THE TEACHER WHAT A BLUE-
print is to a builder. It is a formal, step-by-step
outline that guides the teacher in making his detailed
preparation and his classroom presentation.

To use another illustration, a lesson plan is like a
recipe for a cake. Some of the best cooks never use a
recipe, at least, not one from a book or a card. Their
years of experience and training have made the cake-
making procedure second nature with them. As the
cook moves from one step of the work to another, she
is carefully following a plan, but to the observer she
may appear to be using just a little bit of this and a
little bit of that. The novice has but to try to imitate
her, however, to learn that what appears to be a hit-or-
miss proposition actually calls for a plan as definite as
a written recipe. So with our teaching. Until our plans
or procedures become almost second nature to us, we
need some sort of written outline to follow.

Advantages of Using a Plan

The lesson plan is strictly for the use of the teacher.
No housewife would think of serving her guests a copy
of the recipe with her cake. Nor does the possession of
a lesson plan mean a slavish adherence to it. Occasion-

ally it is necessary to deviate from the lesson plan in order to take advantage of some unforeseen teaching situation. Teaching is by no means an exact science. Instead of curbing the teacher's freedom and initiative, a carefully worked out lesson plan may give the teacher a more confident freedom. If an occasion arises that warrants an excursion into some unplanned area of discussion, the teacher who has a lesson plan need not fear that he will be completely sidetracked. At some convenient point in the excursion he can always return to his schedule.

UNITY, ORDER, AND LOGICAL CONTINUITY ARE ACHIEVED BY FOLLOWING A LESSON PLAN. Each class session becomes a unit related to what has gone before and what is to follow. A sense of completing one discussion and then moving on to another is fostered. Neither the teacher nor the members of the class will be plagued by the feeling of getting nowhere. Although most of us tolerate it, few of us relish disorder. Most people will respond favorably to a well-ordered class session. Good planning will do much to assure such a response.

A PLANNED LESSON IS ALREADY HALF PREPARED. Especially if the teacher does his planning early, material for the various parts of the lesson will fall into place like fruit in the process of being graded will drop into the proper bins. The gathering of much material which later turns out to be unrelated to the lesson will be eliminated automatically. The cook who is following a recipe need not get out everything in the pantry, but only what is required by the recipe. If the lesson is planned at the first of the week, the teacher will know what he is looking for by way of additional material, illustrations, and applications. By the end of the week he will require only a few finishing touches to have his lesson ready to present.

PLANNED LESSONS BUILD THE TEACHER'S CONFIDENCE. He approaches his class fortified with the knowledge that he knows each step that he proposes to take. Even if he should wander from his path he knows that there is a path to which he can return. This confidence on the part of the teacher evokes a similar confidence in the minds of the students. Students appreciate the fact that their teacher knows where he is going and what he is trying to do.

An Outline for a Lesson Plan

A typical lesson plan might be outlined somewhat in the following order:

(1) A statement of purpose
(2) A plan for making the initial contact with the class
(3) A factual introduction
(4) Plans for the presentation of the lesson material
(5) A distinction between primary and secondary issues
(6) Plans for the discussion of the lesson material and the issues
(7) The application of the findings of the discussion
(8) A plan for concluding the discussion in such a way as to indicate the meaning of the lesson in terms of attitudes, action, and policies
(9) A plan for closing the session
(10) A method of introducing the next lesson

Making a Lesson Plan

MAKE YOUR PURPOSE DEFINITE. Is it essential that each class have a specific purpose or set of aims? The objectives of the church school are fairly clear in our minds and each lesson is designed to further those objectives. We aim to develop Christian character, to help people to meet their problems with all the resources of religious faith, and to encourage good churchmanship. Our main objectives are not hard to state, but such general aims are not sufficient to guide us in our preparation and presentation of the lesson. No one will deny the importance of long-range objectives. The more clearly and thoughtfully they are chosen the better. But they are not a substitute for the aims of each particular lesson. Can it be that when we feel we are getting nowhere in our teaching it is because we do not start anywhere? To go anywhere in general or to do anything in general is exceedingly difficult.

A well-formulated set of objectives for a lesson acts like a magnet pushed through a heap of carpet tacks. It attracts to itself lesson materials, illustrations, and discussion questions. The other features of the lesson plan will all take shape around this statement of purpose. Once our aims are defined, the time required for other items of preparation will be greatly reduced and our presentation of the lesson will be direct and clear.

More specifically, what is meant by lesson aims? Are these not set forth by the writers of the lesson materials? In a general way they are, but the purpose for a given lesson with a given class is an individual matter. The teacher is the one who knows the specific needs of the class. He may ask himself, therefore, "What need of the class can best be met by this particular lesson?" "What do I want the members of the class to do after they have studied this lesson?"

Suppose the lesson theme is "Jesus Meets His Enemies." In view of the needs of your class you might state your purpose in this way: "We purpose to develop a working attitude and policy among the members of the class that will help them to succeed in spite of adverse criticism and opposition." If there is a tendency toward grumbling and faultfinding among the students, the lesson might be directed instead toward a solution of that problem. Our purpose might take some such form as this: "I want the students to be positive and constructive in their criticisms."

In most cases the lesson aims will be stated in terms of programs of action. Christian truths need to be worked out in terms of action if they are to be living truths. We may find it helpful to write down several aims for the lesson and to select one from the list which appears to be most appropriate for the group.

With lesson themes that are especially familiar there is a strong tendency to present only the facts of the lesson without pursuing any specific purpose. For example, in a lesson on Jesus's interview with Nicodemus, we could assume that our purpose is merely to review what is already known. But is there any way that we can deal with the lesson so that it will be regarded as "new and significant" by the members of the class? Suppose we know that the members of our class have difficulty in making up their minds to follow the demands that Jesus makes upon them. Their lives run in deep ruts that they are afraid to abandon. Our lesson aim might be to develop decisiveness and independence of judgment in the individual members of the class. We might plan to build the lesson around such questions as, "What prevents people from being able to make up their minds?" "Why are they afraid to strike off on a new course even though they know it is the right one?" Examples of this nature may give the lesson a new turn which will prove both interesting and helpful to the class. Careful thought about purpose is even more essential in the case of a familiar lesson than with one that is less familiar.

PLAN YOUR INITIAL CONTACT. In the old days before airplanes had starters, the motors had to be cranked by hand. Two men were required, one to operate the controls, the other to turn the propeller by hand. The motor was turned over a few times before the ignition was turned on. Then the man at the controls would shout, "Contact!" and the man at the propeller would give it a quick turn. The machine was lifeless until contact was established. In teaching, too, nothing happens or can be expected to happen until we make contact with the minds and the experience of our students.

Making contact, then, is the primary consideration in getting the lesson started. It is a matter of gaining the attention of the members of the class.

Of course there is no point in proceeding with the lesson until we have the students with us. When we take the family for a boatride we do not pull away from the dock until all the passengers are in the boat. Many a teacher has had the embarrassing experience of getting halfway through the lesson only to find that he has left the class behind. Perhaps the only rule that can be given to govern this situation is: Get going as quickly as possible, but make sure that the class is with you. Following are some time-tested methods of establishing this initial contact:

1. *Direct Demand for Attention.* The teacher may depend on his authority to command attention. He may say, "Let us begin now; give me your attention," and proceed to conduct the session like an army officer dealing with his battalion. What about this method of making contact with hospitable minds? Does it create a receptive attitude in the minds of the members of the class? What kind of response is usually given to a command?

Possibly this may seem to be the easiest method to achieve the desired results. However, there are many serious objections to it. It tends to place a barrier between the teacher and the members of his class. The teacher who assumes such authority can scarcely be regarded as an associate or a fellow-searcher after truth. Furthermore, learning is a voluntary experience. As soon as a command is given the elements of free and voluntary participation are crushed. Resentment is almost certain to be aroused. Even though attention may be given for a brief time, it is not likely to endure. In fact, almost any other method of making contact with the minds of the students is to be preferred.

2. *Requesting Attention.* A request for attention may be less objectionable than a command. Much depends upon the teacher's manner and tone of voice.

Usually, however, such a request is merely a command with a question mark. Attention gained in this way will hardly be sustained unless the request is followed immediately by some procedure that attracts and holds the attention. Since the latter is necessary, would it not be better to start with this second procedure?

3. *Using a Focus for Attention.* Almost any kind of object, diagram, or map will serve to attract attention. This method meets with more ready acceptance from small children than from adults, but it is used constantly by advertisers seeking the attention of adults. A missionary speaking on China held up a beautiful handmade Chinese garment, with the result that no command or request for attention was needed. A teacher of young people opened his lesson, "The Cleansing of the Temple" by unrolling a large diagram of the temple courts. He had indicated on the drawing the place where the money-changers sat and the areas where the animals to be used for sacrifices were kept. Members of the class crowded around to see the drawing. Another resourceful teacher brought to a lesson on race relations a photograph of a sign at the approach to a city in Germany which said, *"Juden Verboten"* (Jews Forbidden). As soon as his students saw the picture they wanted to know what the sign meant.

4. *Using an Illustration.* A story, an illustration, or a hypothetical situation may serve the same purpose. Even with adults the words, "Once upon a time," work magic in claiming attention. When Jesus began, "A man was going down from Jerusalem to Jericho," he did not have to say, "Give me your attention, please."

We might try asking what our students would do in some problem situation. For instance: "Suppose you were lost in the woods of northern Maine and you came upon an unoccupied cabin, would you break in and use what you found there until you were rescued? Would you consider this stealing?" Such a situation stimulates imagination. Often it serves better than anything else to establish contact.

A good introduction for the lesson may be provided by a member of the class who has had some noteworthy experience. Suppose the lesson has to do with the observance of a Jewish feast and that one of the students works for a doctor of that faith. The student's contacts with his employer and his family afford him the opportunity to gather authentic information with respect to Jewish customs and practices. To ask that student to make a brief statement of his findings and observations to begin the class session will stimulate the interest of all the members. Perhaps others in the class will have had similar experiences which they can contribute to the discussion.

Sometimes one or more students may be asked to make a report of an interview or visit with the personnel of some special institution such as a rescue mission or a mission school. In starting the lesson with such contributions from students, it is not difficult to gain attention and to relate the lesson to living issues.

Items in the news also provide a good starting-place for a discussion. The teacher will be wise to cut the article from the newspaper and ask some member of the class to read it and give his opinion on it. Then, others in the class may be asked what they think. The teacher should be prepared to lead the discussion from this starting-point into the basic issues of the session.

5. *Using Questions.* Much has been said in this book about the use of questions in teaching. Their usefulness to the teacher who wants to make contact with the minds of his students is obvious. By its very nature a question calls for a response. It represents the most informal ground for the fellowship of kindred minds. Because the use of questions is less spectacular than the other methods suggested, the teacher may use them frequently without seeming to overdo the practice. The sustained popular interest in radio quizzes offers ample testimony to the appeal of questions.

PLAN FOR INTRODUCING THE FACTS OF THE LESSON. Obviously, the purpose of the introduction to the lesson is to help the students to become acquainted with the general topic to be discussed. After the teacher has made contact with the minds of his students, the next step is to establish contact with the lesson theme and material. Unfortunately, to outline and describe this process is far easier than to carry it out. Unless the interest aroused by the initial contact is transferred to the lesson topic the entire effort will be meager in its results. Some of the ways of directing the attention already gained toward the lesson follow.

1. If activities or projects have been assigned, introducing the lesson is merely a matter of setting to work on unfinished business. One of the valuable features of this method of teaching is the continuity of interest which such activities sustain. For instance, if a committee is to report on an interview with the head of the

welfare department concerning the social problems growing out of broken homes, the attention of the class will, of course, be focused upon the problem out of which the assignment grew.

2. When a diagram, chart, or other object has been used to make contact with the class, introducing the lesson will be merely a matter of following through on the original suggestion. For example, the teacher may hold up a check from a Chinese laundry to attract the attention of the class. This very act focuses attention upon the Chinese people. It stimulates questions such as, "What is their religion?" "Are there any Christians in China?" "How did they happen to become Christians?" "Why did Robert Morrison and others take the Christian message to China?" "Why would Jesus want his religion offered to the Chinese?" Thus, by using a quick sequence of questions the topic of Christian missions and world-wide Christianity can be introduced. One last question, "What did Jesus say about offering Christianity to a people like the Chinese?" might be used to introduce the reading of the Scripture.

3. To read the printed text of the Scripture seldom provides an effective introduction. Centuries separate us from the terms and the events in the Scripture record. The transition from our world to the world of the Bible is hard for the student to make. Unless he is given some help he will make no real transition. He will hear and read the words of the Scripture as just so many words. On the other hand, every effort possible needs to be expended to make the reading of the Scripture meaningful. To refer again to the lesson on world-wide Christianity, the reading of the Great Commission will have

more interest and meaning for the members of the class if it is introduced by a sequence of questions like those suggested.

On some rare occasions the reading of Scripture texts or passages may be used to introduce the lesson, but to make this a general practice is to accept the hardly justifiable assumption that the easiest method is always the best.

4. Regardless of the method employed to direct attention to the lesson theme, the teacher will find that the use of questions is exceedingly helpful in getting the job done. If the class is working on a project, a single question or a sequence will serve as a stepping-stone from what has gone before to the material to be presented in the current lesson. Sometimes asking a few questions by way of review will serve to pick up the threads of interest from the preceding lesson and attach them to the lesson at hand.

DECIDE ON A METHOD OF PRESENTING THE LESSON MATERIAL. The presentation of lesson material calls for the use of all the tools at our disposal. Charts, diagrams, maps, filmstrips, slides, committee reports, questions, and illustrations, all may find a place in the presentation of a single lesson. The object is to get the entire sweep of the lesson before the class as quickly and as effectively as possible.

MAKE CERTAIN THAT THE PRIMARY AND SECONDARY ISSUES WHICH YOU WILL WISH TO DISCUSS LATER WILL BE BROUGHT OUT CLEARLY. In fact, you may plan to use them as a kind of outline or framework around which the presentation of the lesson is organized. This represents the raw material which it is our purpose to discuss and to focus upon the lives of our students. Suppose that the lesson is on Peter's denial of Christ. The students need to know the man Peter, and the conditions under which he lived and served. How did he happen to be with Jesus? What did he do before he became a disciple? What did he expect Jesus to do when the soldiers came out to arrest him? Who sent the soldiers? Of necessity, this part of the lesson is more factual than the other portions, yet it does not call for a formal lecture, nor does it mean that the students may not have an active part in it. Although the lecture method may be slightly better than reading from the teacher's or pupil's book or some other piece of printed material, neither method is recommended except perhaps with a very large class.

In calling attention to the leading issues presented by the lesson, a current news story or community event may serve to bring them into focus. Suppose we are teaching a lesson on the book of Jonah. What are the main issues in the book? Jonah was too narrow in his views. His prejudices against the people of a different race were so deep that he could not rejoice in the evidence he saw that God's mercy was being shown them. He was so angry and unhappy that he wanted to die. In presenting these basic issues of the lesson, introduce a new item, telling of racial hatred and of injustice inflicted upon a minority group. This will bring to life within the experience of the class the ancient story of Jonah.

We may persuade the students to help us analyze the lesson material and set down on the blackboard the leading issues in four or five brief statements, making sure that the issue we wish to point up in the conclusion of the lesson is discovered by the students during the course of the analysis. We may find it necessary to ask several questions before we can lead the class to uncover this issue. But the very fact that we have arrived at the point together will give it freshness and added force for our students. When the discovery is made it should be vigorously outlined so that it will stand out. In the case of the lesson on Jonah the point might be stated thus: "God is not pleased with narrowness and prejudice." Or, "Those who cannot appreciate the good things that come to other people are likely to be unhappy."

UPON THE BASIS OF THIS ANALYSIS WE MAY BE ABLE TO PLAN TO CONDUCT A LIVELY DISCUSSION. We need to know how we propose to move from one question to another, from one issue to the next. Events may take place which will lead the group into other fields of exploration, but to have a plan will give unity and point to the discussion.

THE NEXT STEP IN THE LESSON PLAN WILL BE CONCERNED WITH THE QUESTION, "WHAT DOES THE DISCUSSION OF THESE ISSUES HAVE TO DO WITH US?" It is the old question which in our slang is expressed by "So what?" For instance, "What does Peter's denial of Christ have to do with our situation today?" would lead to a present-day application of the lesson on Peter's denial of Christ. The consideration of various possible and helpful applications may reach outward in many directions. Suggestions from members of the class as to possible applications of the lesson will be valuable. It is in this part of the lesson study that our original purpose will begin to take shape.

THE CONCLUSION OF A LESSON NEEDS TO BE MORE CARE-FULLY PLANNED THAN ANY OTHER PORTION. This is the place to clinch the truths of the lesson for the lives of our students. Concluding the lesson is like wrapping up a package so that it may be carried away. The conclusion gathers together the leading applications of the lesson and brings them to focus upon the lives of the students.

The teacher will do well to ask himself the question, "What do I want the students to do about this study?" If the answer is, "I want them to commit their lives to a definite program of action," then he will plan his conclusion to achieve that end. Before actually finishing our plans for concluding the session, we may find it helpful to go back to our stated purpose.

It is important for us to plan so that we do not run out of time before we reach our conclusion, for if we do, considerable time and effort will go for nothing. We will be in the position of a salesman who does not have time to get his customer's signature on the dotted line. If some part of the planned lesson has to be cut, let it be anything but the conclusion. This is not to say that the conclusion needs to be long. It should be as brief as possible without appearing to be hurried and there-fore of minor significance. Often a few short sentences of summary and a question or two will suffice. We are anxious to get a response to our conclusion. Brevity will give the suggestion of decisiveness. Our conclusion should be brief and to the point.

PLAN A DEFINITE CLOSING. One of the most common diseases that infect our conclusions is generality. It is easy to let a fine lesson end in vague or pious-sounding exhortations. Yet, people do not do things in general, they do particular things. If action is the purpose of the lesson study, to list a few things which the class *might* do is not definite enough to solicit action. A more definite proposition will stand a much better chance of being adopted by the members of the class. Vagueness is to be avoided as if it were poison in any and all parts of the lesson, but its destructiveness is at its worst when it slips into the conclusion!

THINK ABOUT INTRODUCING THE NEXT LESSON. Thought given to introducing the next Sunday's lesson will make the next week's assignment of teaching just so much easier and more interesting. To announce the topic calls for no special plan, but if our purpose is to arouse interest in what is offered in the next lesson, this part of our lesson plan will be more specific. To throw out some interesting question about the next lesson or to give a brief statement of a problem that it presents may serve to stimulate interest. Assignments of committee work or other announced plans of activity to be carried on in connection with the next lesson or lessons will be effective. Curiosity is an ever-present friend of the teacher. To appeal to the curiosity of the students will be to help to introduce the next lesson effectively.

Part Three: IN THE CLASSROOM

O young and fearless Prophet
Of ancient Galilee:
Thy life is still a summons
To serve humanity,
To make our thoughts and actions
Less prone to please the crowd,
To stand with humble courage
For truth, with hearts uncowed.

We marvel at the purpose
That held Thee to Thy course
While ever on the hilltop
Before Thee loomed the cross;
Thy steadfast face set forward
Where love and duty shone,
While we betray so quickly
And leave Thee there alone.

Create in us the splendor
That dawns when hearts are kind,
That knows not race nor station
As boundaries of the mind;
That learns to value beauty,
In heart, or brain, or soul,
And longs to bind God's children
Into one perfect whole.

—S. RALPH HARLOW

8

Getting the Job Done

◇◇

ARE WE TO ASSUME FROM WHAT HAS BEEN SAID THUS far that if we employ proper methods and procedures in teaching, we will eliminate all the problems that arise in conducting a church school class? By no means! Instead, the methods which have been suggested here will give rise to a special group of problems for the teacher. Often the dread of facing these problems discourages a new teacher from launching out upon the more adventurous types of teaching. Perhaps it will be well to discuss here some of the difficulties which we may expect to encounter if we follow the suggestions offered in the earlier chapters of this book.

Keeping Order

A highly formal type of classroom procedure will tend to produce a maximum of order. Adults, especially those who are accustomed to formal services and lectures, will submit readily enough to the demands of a highly formal situation. They may pay no real attention to what is going on, or receive no special benefit from the session, but there will be little if any evidence of disorder. Young people respond a little less favorably than adults to the demands of a formal situation, but still they do respond.

If order were the supreme value to be sought in teaching, the more stiff and formal our sessions the better. Order is indeed both necessary and desirable, but it is by no means the chief value that we seek.

As we relax the formality of our classroom procedure in the interest of other objectives, the problem of order comes to the fore. In a spirited discussion it is not uncommon for several people to be talking at once. Work on projects may create an appearance of confusion. As the members of the class move about or discuss their efforts, there will be a measure of disorder. Observers of this type of classroom procedure are likely to conclude that everyone is doing only what appeals to him. Not only can they not hear a pin drop, they may even fail to hear a book drop!

The problem for the teacher is to determine the minimum amount of order that is essential and then to maintain that minimum. General confusion, of course, will destroy the effectiveness of the entire class effort, but too much insistence upon order will kill the spirit of the class sessions.

The problem is not really so difficult as it may appear. If the session has a clear purpose, is well planned, and elicits the keen interest of the class, it will foster an order of its own. The teacher will need only to keep the session moving along toward its completion. Occasionally, he may need to step in and refocus the attention of the students or redirect their activities. Often he can accomplish this by asking a question or giving a summarizing statement that gathers up the loose ends of the discussion.

Confusion in a classroom usually reflects the loss of a

sense of direction, so that to re-establish order we re-introduce the element of direction. We might formulate a guiding principle for ourselves as follows: Insist upon maintaining only the amount of order needed to get the work of the class done without discouraging free discussion and activity among the members of the class and without recourse to formality or the use of coercion.

Those Who Do All the Talking

What are we to do when one or two persons monopolize the discussion; if, when a question is raised they snap out the answer before anyone else has a chance to think? It makes little practical difference whether their answers are right or wrong, they deprive the other members of the class of the opportunity to enter into the discussion. Soon the latter become content merely to observe what is going on in the class, neither wishing nor expecting to have any active part in it. What can we do to avoid this kind of situation?

Definite assignments given to the less aggressive members of the class will help to bring them into the discussion. If we see to it that even one member of this group is fortified with the results of some special research that has been assigned to him, he will cease to be disposed to sit by and see his less well-informed neighbors take over the discussion. Or, when the monopolizers insist upon taking over, as they sometimes do, the teacher may call on the person who has done the special assignment, thus bringing a new voice into the discussion.

Happy is the teacher who knows his students well enough to direct his questions to individuals by name. If the person designated is unable to answer, the teacher still may foil the monopolizer by rephrasing the question and persisting in giving help in other ways until the appointed individual gives the proper answer. By pursuing such a policy, even at the cost of ignoring the other members of the class temporarily, the teacher will soon be able to establish a pattern for the class discussions that will ensure general participation.

Another way to curb the monopolizer is occasionally to submit his answers to the other members of the class for their judgment. When he sees that he has answered hastily and without sound reasoning, he may be moved to take more time to think about the next question.

Thorough preparation, experience, and a sympathetic knowledge of the individual members of his class on the part of the teacher will help him to get the broadest possible participation of his students in class activities. He will find that some students are quicker than others; yet, often those students who appear to be the slowest or least responsive have most to contribute. Too often the ready talker is shallow rather than thoughtful.

When Everyone Talks at Once

Perhaps the class sometimes goes to the opposite extreme, when everyone wants to talk at once, when private arguments break out among the students, and there is general confusion. A teacher who has been trying for weeks to get a spirited discussion going may be embarrassed by such a situation. He may feel like a man drilling for water who at last strikes a supply so abundant that he is unable to handle it.

However embarrassing, this situation is a good sign. Nonetheless it presents a real problem. How can we restore sufficient order to make effective use of this interest and enthusiasm? There are several methods:

1. We may suggest a roll call of class opinion, first giving each person an opportunity to state his views, and then taking up the various statements in order.

2. If the teacher is able to discern the real issue behind the arguments, he may clear the atmosphere by putting it into words and calling for a discussion of it.

3. If the private arguments involve irrelevant items, the teacher may call upon one of the arguers to show how his argument relates itself to the class discussion.

The important thing is for the teacher to re-establish order in the class session without discouraging the enthusiasm and participation of the members of his class. Almost anything is better than a dull class session, or one where the teacher is the sole participant.

Differences of Opinion

Sometimes rather sharp differences of opinion may arise between the teacher and one or more of his students. Free and spirited discussion tends to bring any such differences to the surface. However, when the work of the class has reached a high level of mutual respect between the teacher and his students, these differences in point of view need not hinder the progress of the discussion. Naturally, the teacher will want to set forth his position to the best advantage. At the same time he may need to guard against any feeling of frustration, ill-feeling, or embarrassment that may arise through his differences with his students. How easy it is for a teacher to become authoritative or even dogmatic without ever intending it when his favorite ideas are challenged!

When a reasonable amount of time and effort has been expended in an effort to gain agreement, the issue should be dropped in such a way that the class understands the teacher's position. The group still may not agree with the teacher, but they will respect his fairness and his conviction. To allow a controversy of this kind to disintegrate until it becomes a matter of personalities and personal loyalties is obviously a grievous mistake. But this can happen far more easily than one might imagine. Good will and fellowship are far more valuable than total agreement upon any issue.

Controversial Issues

What shall we do with highly controversial issues? Is it wise to avoid them? Shall we dodge them, or shall we simply dismiss them as soon as they are raised? We can hardly hope to achieve a wholesome fellowship of truth-seeking if we persist in avoiding any issue that may arise. A teacher cannot achieve a reputation for sincerity, fairness, and honesty if he makes it a practice to play hide and seek with controversial issues. Certainly it is essential that the teacher be respected for his sincerity, fairness, and honest dealing with the truth. Such a reputation will hardly be enhanced by his avoidance of difficult questions. Even though valuable time may be consumed in a class discussion of controversial matters, a teacher cannot afford to rule them out.

When issues are controversial simply because they are alive and crucial, they may offer a splendid teaching opportunity. They have the qualities of timeliness and great potential interest. The teacher can use such issues to stimulate active participation on the part of the members of his class. Used thus, they serve as contact-makers for issues more specifically related to the lesson theme. For example, if the lesson concerns social justice as preached by the prophet Amos, the teacher might raise the question, "What do you think of the exploitation of the backward peoples of the world by commercial interests in the name of good business?" or, "What is meant by a legitimate profit in business?" "Does keeping within the law mean acting justly?" With most groups such questions can be depended on to get things started.

Before setting forth on an adventure with questions such as this, the teacher needs to be prepared to direct the discussion toward a helpful study of what justice means in terms of individuals and groups. To be sure, there is far more risk involved in this approach than in a purely historical study of the herdsman-prophet. The students may become so excited about the subject that they will all want to talk at once. Can there actually be any real question as to the relative values of these two procedures for teaching? What teacher is concerned merely with avoiding risks? Teaching is an *adventure* with people!

Covering the Whole Lesson

Reducing the formality of the class procedure makes it difficult to maintain the desired balance between time and material. It is easy to get interested in some question more or less remotely connected with the lesson and to spend the entire period discussing it. In using a prepared manuscript it is possible to have one's presentation timed to the second. Even with a lecture the problem of timing is not especially difficult. But when we adopt a more informal procedure, a great deal of practice, not to mention trial and error, is required to keep the session properly balanced and timed.

The worst of it is that two essential steps in our lesson plan are the most likely to suffer—application and conclusion. As we have said earlier, these are of supreme importance to the effectiveness of our classwork. Perhaps the only way for us to avoid the predicament of running out of time is to plan the session carefully with a time-schedule in mind and to check the time occasionally as the class activities proceed. When planned events must be left out, let them be dropped in some one of the steps ahead of the two important final steps in our teaching.

Getting Assignments Done

Is there any way to get students to carry out assignments? It may seem that there is not. Many teachers have simply given up. They no longer even try. Others keep on trying because they feel that they must, although they have given up any hope of achieving real success. Is this to be our final solution of the problem? If so, we have not really solved it, we have surrendered to it. What can we do to persuade students to apply themselves to assignments? Here are some suggestions that may be helpful:

We must recognize that homework is not generally popular, especially with school-age young people. Any assignments which resemble regular homework will hardly be received with enthusiasm. Therefore, we must make assignments of a different sort. Much of the outside work which we want school-age young people to do, and which they need to do, may take the form of interviews with specific persons. Or, if a member of your class is gifted or even merely interested in some particular field, let him work along those lines. For instance, a student who is keen about mechanical drawing will be a good person to help on charts, diagrams, and other drawings. Someone else in the class who delights in politics might take on an assignment in that area without resenting it as homework. A teacher following some such plan as this is often amazed at the amount of work that his students will do outside of the class sessions. Its value in teaching can hardly be exaggerated.

We may set forth some simple principles here to govern this situation:

(1) Never give up trying.

(2) Exploit to the full any interests shown by any of the individual members of the class.

(3) Make generous use of assigned material in conducting the class.

(4) Let those who fail to do their assignments feel that they have failed both themselves and the class. In this connection, any form of scolding or abuse is inappropriate. Teachers are often strongly tempted to register their disappointment too vigorously, and students quickly build up resentment toward such treatment.

Human curiosity is the teacher's ever-present ally. If we can arouse the curiosity of the student with respect to some point in the coming Sunday's lesson, he may be persuaded to study it, or at least enough of it to assuage his curiosity. People really like to learn once they have overcome the inertia of their pre-occupations of one kind or another. Observe the eagerness people display over finding the solution to a puzzle, or their impatience to learn the outcome of some athletic contest. When a small crowd gathers on a street corner, it is only a short time until dozens of other curious people are pushing and staring to find out what the attraction is. Curiosity supplies strong motivation. If we can stimulate it in our students, they will apply themselves outside of the classroom. Even a small measure of success in this respect is worth all the effort we can put into it.

This rather obvious word might be added. People can be persuaded to do things that appeal to them as being worth while or to their advantage. It is well for us to keep this in mind as we select and make assignments. When we convince our students that doing outside work is important for them as well as for the class, success with assignments will be assured. Usually it is wiser to try to do this indirectly. Most lectures from teachers on the value of doing outside work meet with considerable resistance. To tell a story of how one or two students have found it to their advantage to carry out a class assignment will carry the point far more effectively.

Using Our Mistakes

No one can teach a class without making mistakes! In any adventure there is an element of risk, and teaching is no exception. Mistakes do not, or need not, represent complete losses. Instead, they may become exceedingly useful to the teacher. For this reason one of the most important phases of a teacher's schedule has to do with mistakes.

The wise teacher develops a practical program of some kind for detecting his mistakes. Then he can determine the causes for them and profit from them to the fullest extent in planning his future efforts. In short, some form of post-session checkup needs to be devised. Perhaps the simplest kind of checkup is a mental review of what went on in the class session, carried out while the events of the lesson are fresh in the teacher's mind. This procedure may be facilitated by using a brief schedule for evaluation, such as the one presented on the following page.

Of course more detailed plans and schedules of evaluation may be employed. Each section of the lesson plan may be checked by a series of questions. Highly trained teachers may find it helpful to follow a teacher's score sheet similar to those used by public school supervisors. Here, each section of the session is graded excellent, good, fair, poor, and so on.

Naturally it is difficult for anyone to grade his own work, but there is considerable value in the effort to do so. What concerns us as church school teachers is to find the method of procedure that will best enable us to make the fullest use of our mistakes. Perhaps each teacher must seek to discover a plan of post-session checkup that fits his own personal needs and temperament.

God has given us a great work to do in our teaching. Ours is a thrilling adventure with people. To render an acceptable account of our stewardship is the goal of our striving. Mistakes and failures may both chasten us in our pride and guide us toward greater effectiveness. The assurance that we are co-workers with the Master Teacher is our constant inspiration and our sure reward.

A Schedule for Self-Evaluation

(1) *Interest*

How much interest did the teacher evidence? How much did the students show? What were the points of greatest interest? What portions of the session were the dullest? What made the difference between the intensity of interest in these portions?

(2) *Participation*

How many students took active part in the discussion? Was participation spontaneous? Did it further the purpose of the session? At what points did the participation lag? Were there any obvious reasons for this? What important bits of information about the students and their problems became apparent from the discussion?

(3) *Effectiveness*

Did the session proceed according to plan? How many of the students really got the point or points of the lesson? Did the discussion help the students to lay claim to the leading themes of the lesson? What was the response to the illustrations? Did they make the points clear? What was the response to the discussion questions? Did they actually serve to open the minds of the students? Which questions were the most stimulating? Which missed the mark? Did the application and the conclusion take hold of the students? Did the discussion lead to a program of action?